CW00839768

Easy Pear Cookbook

50 Delicious Pear Recipes

By
BookSumo Press
All rights reserved

Published by
http://www.booksumo.com

ENJOY THE RECIPES?

KEEP ON COOKING
WITH 6 MORE FREE COOKBOOKS!

Visit our website and simply enter your email address to join the club and receive your 6 cookbooks.

http://booksumo.com/magnet

https://www.instagram.com/booksumopress/

https://www.facebook.com/booksumo/

LEGAL NOTES

All Rights Reserved. No Part Of This Book May Be Reproduced Or Transmitted In Any Form Or By Any Means. Photocopying, Posting Online, And / Or Digital Copying Is Strictly Prohibited Unless Written Permission Is Granted By The Book's Publishing Company. Limited Use Of The Book's Text Is Permitted For Use In Reviews Written For The Public.

Table of Contents

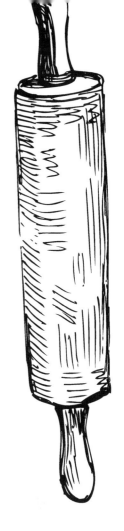

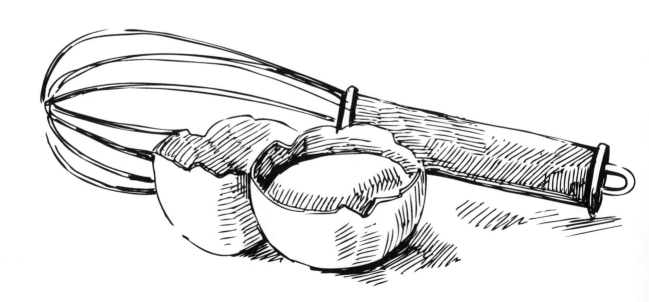

Wendy's
Pear Vinaigrette

Prep Time: 10 mins
Total Time: 10 mins

Servings per Recipe: 12	
Calories	101 kcal
Fat	9 g
Cholesterol	3.6g
Sodium	0.1 g
Carbohydrates	0 mg
Protein	60 mg

Ingredients

1 ripe pear - peeled, cored, and chopped
1/2 C. white wine
1 clove garlic, chopped
2 tsp Dijon mustard
1/4 C. white balsamic vinegar
1 tsp ground black pepper
1/4 tsp sea salt

1/2 C. olive oil

Directions

1. In a blender, add the pear, white wine, garlic, Dijon mustard, white balsamic vinegar, sea salt and black pepper and pulse till well combined.
2. While the motor is running slowly, add the olive oil and pulse till the salad dressing is thick and creamy.

HOT PEAR
Relish

Prep Time: 30 mins
Total Time: 3 hrs 10 mins

Servings per Recipe: 192
Calories	19 kcal
Fat	0.1 g
Carbohydrates	4.6g
Protein	0.2 g
Cholesterol	0 mg
Sodium	52 mg

Ingredients

12 large pears
3 large onions, coarsely chopped
3 large green bell peppers, seeded and coarsely chopped
4 jalapeno peppers, coarsely chopped
2 C. apple cider vinegar

2 C. white sugar
9 oz. prepared mustard
1 tbsp salt
10 (1 pint) canning jars with lids and rings, or as needed

Directions

1. In a soup pan, add the pears and enough water to cover.
2. Bring to boil and cook for about 20 minutes.
3. Drain well and keep aside to cool.
4. After cooling, peel, core, and coarsely chop.
5. In a food processor, add the pears, onions, green bell peppers, and jalapeño peppers into a food processor and pulse till chopped finely.
6. Add the vinegar, sugar, prepared mustard and salt into the pear mixture and bring to a boil.
7. Reduce the heat to medium-low and simmer for about 1 hour.
8. Sterilize the jars and lids in boiling water for at least 5 minutes.
9. Place the pear relish into the hot, sterilized jars, filling the jars to within 1/4 inch of the top.
10. Run a knife around the insides of the jars after they have been filled to remove any air bubbles.
11. With a moist paper towel, wipe the rims of the jars to remove any food residue.
12. Top with the lids and screw on the rings.
13. Arrange a rack in the bottom of a large pan and fill halfway with the water.

14. Bring to a boil over high heat, then carefully, place the jars into the pan using a holder.
15. Leave a 2-inch space between the jars.
16. Pour in more boiling water if necessary until the water level is at least 1 inch above the tops of the jars.
17. Bring the water to a full boil.
18. Cover the pan and process for about 20 minutes.
19. Remove the jars from the pan and keep aside to cool.
20. After cooling, press the top of each lid with a finger, ensuring that the seal is tight.
21. Store in a cool and dark place.

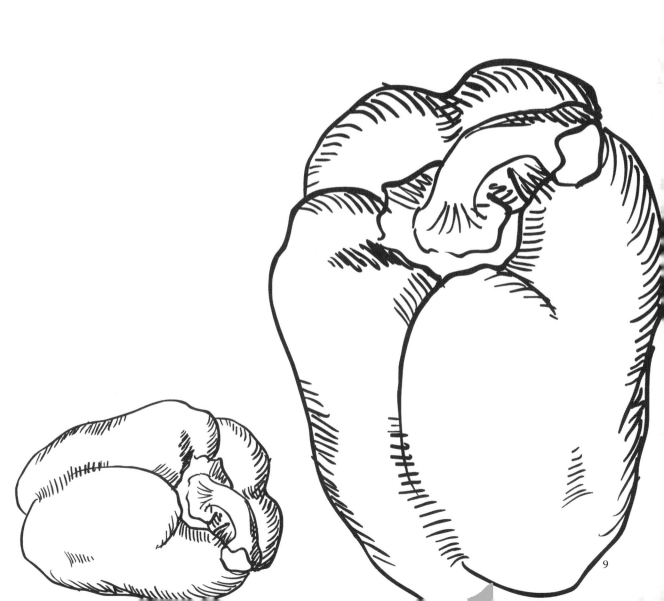

NEW HAMPSHIRE
Pear Honey

Prep Time: 45 mins
Total Time: 3 hrs 45 mins

Servings per Recipe: 64
Calories   111 kcal
Fat   0 g
Carbohydrates   28.7g
Protein   0.1 g
Cholesterol   0 mg
Sodium   1 mg

Ingredients

8 C. peeled, cored and chopped pears
1 C. unsweetened pineapple juice
8 C. white sugar

Directions

1. In a large pan, add the pears, pineapple juice and sugar on medium-high heat.
2. Bring to a boil, stirring occasionally.
3. Reduce the heat to medium and cook, stirring for about 2-3 hours or mixture looks like honey.
4. Transfer the mixture into the sterile jars, filling about within 1/4-inch of the top.
5. With a clean damp cloth, wipe the rims and seal the jars with the lids and rings.
6. Process in a boiling water canner for 10 minutes.

Bonnie's Best
Bartlett Pie

Prep Time: 15 mins
Total Time: 1 hr

Servings per Recipe: 8

Calories	431 kcal
Fat	25.8 g
Carbohydrates	47.6g
Protein	4.5 g
Cholesterol	66 mg
Sodium	369 mg

Ingredients

1 (9 inch) unbaked pie crust
3 C. sliced Bartlett pears
1 C. sour cream
1/2 C. white sugar
2 tbsp all-purpose flour
1 egg
1/2 tsp vanilla extract
1/2 tsp salt

Topping:
1/2 C. all-purpose flour
1/2 C. butter
1/4 C. white sugar
1 tsp ground cinnamon

Directions

1. Set your oven to 400 degrees F before doing anything else.
2. Press the pie crust into a 9-inch pie dish.
3. Arrange the pear slices in the pie crust.
4. In a bowl, mix together the sour cream, 1/2 C. of the sugar, 2 tbsp of the flour, egg, vanilla extract and salt.
5. Place the sour cream mixture over the pear slices.
6. For topping in a bowl, add 1/2 C. of the flour, butter, 1/4 C. of the sugar and cinnamon and mix till it resembles to a coarse crumbs.
7. Cook in the oven for about 35 minutes.
8. Sprinkle the topping over the pie and cook for about 10 minutes more.

PATTY'S
Panos of Pears

🍲 Prep Time: 15 mins
🕐 Total Time: 1 hr 15 mins

Servings per Recipe: 8
Calories   123 kcal
Fat   0.1 g
Carbohydrates   28.6g
Protein   0.3 g
Cholesterol   0 mg
Sodium   1 mg

Ingredients

4 Bosc pears, halved and cored
1/2 C. white sugar
1/4 tsp vanilla extract

1/4 C. Cointreau or other orange liqueur

Directions

1. In a large pan, add the pears.
2. Add the enough water to cover the pears by 1 inch.
3. Stir in the sugar and bring to a boil.
4. Cook for about 1 hour or till the liquid has reduced into a light syrup.
5. Remove from the heat and stir in the vanilla.
6. Keep aside to cool till just warm.
7. Stir in the liqueur and serve.

How to Bake
Pears

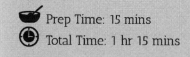

Prep Time: 15 mins

Total Time: 1 hr 15 mins

Servings per Recipe: 4

Calories	206 kcal
Fat	8.9 g
Carbohydrates	34.5g
Protein	0.8 g
Cholesterol	23 mg
Sodium	64 mg

Ingredients

4 Bosc pears
2 tbsp honey
3 tbsp butter, melted

dash ground ginger
1/2 tsp lavender flowers

Directions

1. Set your oven to 375 degrees F before doing anything else.
2. Peel the pears and carefully, scoop out the bottom core.
3. Carefully, cut a small slice from the bottom so pears will stand upright.
4. Arrange the pears in a shallow baking dish.
5. In a microwave safe bowl, add the butter and microwave till melted completely.
6. Pour the melted butter and honey over the pear slices and sprinkle with the ground ginger and lavender.
7. With foil, cover with aluminum foil with the stems poking through foil.
8. Cook in the oven for about 1 hour, basting with released juices occasionally.

MOCK
Fruity Hot Pockets

Prep Time: 15 mins
Total Time: 25 mins

Servings per Recipe: 4	
Calories	387 kcal
Fat	25 g
Carbohydrates	29g
Protein	11.7 g
Cholesterol	15 mg
Sodium	602 mg

Ingredients

cooking spray
1 (8 oz.) package refrigerated crescent rolls
1/4 C. peanut butter, divided
1 Asian pear, chopped - divided

1 tsp ground cinnamon, divided
1/2 C. shredded Cheddar cheese, divided

Directions

1. Set your oven to 375 degrees F before doing anything else and grease a baking sheet.
2. Combine the two crescent roll triangles by overlapping the seams, creating a square.
3. Repeat with the remaining dough to form 4 squares total.
4. Spread 1 tbsp of the peanut butter in the center of each square and top each with the pieces of Asian pear.
5. Sprinkle 1/4 tsp of the cinnamon over the pear slices and top with the Cheddar cheese.
6. Fold one corner of a square over to cover the fillings completely, creating a triangle and seal the edges together.
7. Repeat with the remaining squares.
8. Place the pear pockets on the prepared baking sheet.
9. Cook in the oven for about 10-15 minutes.

Weeknight
Pear Fritters

Prep Time: 15 mins
Total Time: 30 mins

Servings per Recipe: 4
Calories	348 kcal
Fat	27.1 g
Carbohydrates	23.2g
Protein	4.3 g
Cholesterol	47 mg
Sodium	258 mg

Ingredients

1 tbsp olive oil
1 pear - peeled, cored and diced
2/3 C. all-purpose flour
1 tsp baking powder
1/4 tsp salt

1/8 tsp black pepper
1 egg
3 tbsp milk
oil for deep frying

Directions

1. In a skillet, heat oil on medium-high heat.
2. Add the pears and sauté till caramelized.
3. Remove from the heat and keep aside to cool.
4. Meanwhile, in a medium bowl mix together the flour, baking powder salt and pepper.
5. Make a well in the center of the flour mixture.
6. In another small bowl, add the egg and milk and beat well.
7. Add the egg mixture into the flour mixture and mix till well combined.
8. Gently fold in the pears.
9. Heat the oil in a deep fryer to 350 degrees F.
10. With a rounded spoonfuls, place the mixture into the hot oil and fry till golden brown.
11. Transfer onto a paper towel to drain.
12. Serve hot.

EASY-TO-MAKE
Jam

Prep Time: 20 mins
Total Time: 1 hr 35 mins

Servings per Recipe: 4
Calories	99 kcal
Fat	0.1 g
Carbohydrates	25.4g
Protein	0.1 g
Cholesterol	1 mg
Sodium	1 mg

Ingredients

4 1/2 C. mashed ripe pears
3 tbsp powdered fruit pectin
1 tsp ground cinnamon
1/2 tsp ground cloves
1/2 tsp ground allspice
1/2 tsp ground nutmeg
1/4 C. lemon juice
7 1/2 C. white sugar

1 tsp butter
8 half-pint canning jars with lids and rings, or as needed

Directions

1. In a large heavy pan, mix together the pears, fruit pectin, cinnamon, cloves, allspice, nutmeg and lemon juice.
2. Bring to a boil, stirring continuously.
3. Add the sugar, stirring and bring to a full rolling boil.
4. Boil for about 1 minute.
5. Add the butter and mix till foamy.
6. Sterilize the jars and lids in boiling water for at least 5 minutes.
7. Place the pear jam into the hot, sterilized jars, filling the jars to within 1/4 inch of the top.
8. Run a knife around the insides of the jars after they have been filled to remove any air bubbles.
9. With a moist paper towel, wipe the rims of the jars to remove any food residue. Top everything with the lids, and screw on the rings.
10. Arrange a rack in the bottom of a large pan and fill halfway with the water.
11. Bring to a boil and place the jars into the boiling water using a holder, leave a 2-inch space between the jars.

12. Add more boiling water if necessary to bring the water level to at least 1 inch above the tops of the jars.
13. Bring the water to a rolling boil, cover the pan and process for about 10 minutes.
14. Remove the jars from the pan and place onto a cloth-covered surface, several inches apart to cool.
15. After cooling, press the top of each lid with a finger, ensuring that the seal is tight.
16. Store in a cool and dark area.

ARTISANAL
Pear Scones

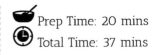

Prep Time: 20 mins
Total Time: 37 mins

Servings per Recipe: 8	
Calories	244 kcal
Fat	10.3 g
Carbohydrates	34.2g
Protein	4.2 g
Cholesterol	49 mg
Sodium	195 mg

Ingredients

1 3/4 C. all-purpose flour
1/3 C. packed brown sugar
2 tsp baking powder
1/2 tsp ground cinnamon
1 pinch salt
1/3 C. butter, chilled

1 egg
1/2 C. half-and-half cream
1 C. chopped pear

Directions

1. Set your oven to 375 degrees F before doing anything else.
2. In a large bowl, sift together the flour, brown sugar, baking powder, cinnamon and salt.
3. With a pastry cutter, cut the butter and mix till a crumbly mixture forms.
4. In another bowl, add the egg and half-and-half and beat well.
5. Add the egg mixture into the flour mixture and mix till well combined.
6. Fold in the pear.
7. With large spoonfuls, place the dough onto an ungreased baking sheet.
8. Cook in the oven for about 15 minutes.
9. Place on a cooling rack before serving.

Summer Night
Poached Pears

🥣 Prep Time: 1 hr
🕐 Total Time: 1 hr 45 mins

Servings per Recipe: 4

Calories	542 kcal
Fat	8.8 g
Carbohydrates	104.7g
Protein	2.5 g
Cholesterol	0 mg
Sodium	13 mg

Ingredients

1/2 (750 milliliter) bottle champagne
1 C. orange juice
1 C. white sugar
4 slices orange
4 whole cloves

1 tsp vanilla extract
4 pears, peeled with stems intact
2/3 C. semisweet chocolate chips

Directions

1. In a pan, mix together the champagne, orange juice and sugar, orange slices, cloves and vanilla on medium heat.
2. Bring to a boil, stirring continuously till the sugar dissolves.
3. Add the pears and reduce the heat.
4. Simmer, covered for about 15 minutes.
5. Uncover and simmer for about 30 minutes more.
6. Remove the pears from the liquid and keep aside to cool.
7. Heat the chocolate in a bowl over hot water, stirring until melted completely.
8. Place the chocolate over the pears and serve.

CINNAMON SUGAR
Pear Cake

Prep Time: 30 mins
Total Time: 1 hr 30 mins

Servings per Recipe: 8

Calories	325 kcal
Fat	12.1 g
Carbohydrates	50g
Protein	5.9 g
Cholesterol	79 mg
Sodium	289 mg

Ingredients

4 eggs
1 1/2 C. packed brown sugar
3/4 C. butter, melted
2 tsp vanilla extract
1 1/2 C. all-purpose flour
1 1/2 C. whole wheat flour
1 C. rolled oats
1 tbsp baking powder

1/2 tsp baking soda
1 1/2 tsp ground cinnamon
1/4 tsp salt
1 1/2 C. coarsely grated unpeeled pears

Directions

1. Set your oven to 325 degrees F before doing anything else and grease and flour a tube pan.
2. In a bowl, mix together the flours, oats, baking powder, baking soda, cinnamon and salt.
3. In another large bowl, add the eggs.
4. Slowly, add the brown sugar and beat till the mixture becomes thick.
5. Add the melted butter and vanilla and beat well.
6. Add the flour mixture into the egg mixture and mix till well combined.
7. Stir in the grated pears.
8. Transfer the mixture in the prepared tube pan evenly.
9. Cook in the oven for about 70 minutes or till a toothpick inserted in the center comes out clean.
10. Transfer cake to a rack to cool.

California Pear Salad

🥣 Prep Time: 20 mins
🕐 Total Time: 30 mins

Servings per Recipe: 6	
Calories	426 kcal
Fat	31.6 g
Carbohydrates	33.1g
Protein	8 g
Cholesterol	21 mg
Sodium	654 mg

Ingredients

1 head leaf lettuce, torn into bite-size pieces
3 pears - peeled, cored and chopped
5 oz. Roquefort cheese, crumbled
1 avocado - peeled, pitted, and diced
1/2 C. thinly sliced green onions
1/4 C. white sugar
1/2 C. pecans

1/3 C. olive oil
3 tbsp red wine vinegar
1 1/2 tsp white sugar
1 1/2 tsp prepared mustard
1 clove garlic, chopped
1/2 tsp salt
fresh ground black pepper to taste

Directions

1. In a skillet, mix together 1/4 C. of the sugar and pecans on medium heat.
2. Cook, stirring gently till the sugar has melted and caramelized the pecans.
3. Transfer pecans onto a waxed paper and keep aside to cool.
4. Then break the pecans into pieces.
5. For the dressing in a bowl, add the oil, vinegar, 1 1/2 tsp of the sugar, mustard, chopped garlic, salt and pepper and beat till well combined.
6. In a large serving bowl, layer the lettuce, pears, blue cheese, avocado and green onions.
7. Pour the dressing over the salad and sprinkle with pecans and serve.

HOW TO MAKE
Pear Butter

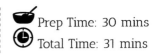

Prep Time: 30 mins
Total Time: 31 mins

Servings per Recipe: 32
Calories	82 kcal
Fat	0.1 g
Carbohydrates	21.5g
Protein	0.2 g
Cholesterol	0 mg
Sodium	1 mg

Ingredients

4 lb. medium pears, quartered and cored
2 C. sugar
1 tsp grated orange zest

1/4 tsp ground nutmeg
1/4 C. orange juice

Directions

1. In a large pan, add the pears on medium heat.
2. Add just enough water to cover the bottom of the pan, about 1/2 cup.
3. Cook for about 30 minutes.
4. Press the pears through a sieve and measure out 2 quarts of the pulp.
5. In a large pan, add the pear pulp and sugar and stir to dissolve the sugar on medium heat.
6. Stir in the orange zest, nutmeg and orange juice.
7. Cook till the mixture is thick enough to mound in a spoon.
8. Cook, stirring occasionally for about 1 hour.
9. Transfer the pear butter into the hot sterile jars, leaving 1/4 inch of head space.
10. Remove the air bubbles by sliding a metal spatula around where the pear butter touches the glass.
11. Wipe the jar rims clean and seal with the lids and rings.
12. Process for 10 minutes in a boiling water bath.

Peachy and Pears
Fruity Salsa

Prep Time: 15 mins
Total Time: 30 mins

Servings per Recipe: 8
Calories	76 kcal
Fat	1.8 g
Carbohydrates	16g
Protein	0.3 g
Cholesterol	0 mg
Sodium	3 mg

Ingredients

1 tbsp olive oil
1/2 red onion, diced
2 cloves garlic, minced
4 peaches - pitted and diced
1 pear - peeled, cored, and diced

1/4 C. honey
1 tsp curry powder
salt and pepper to taste

Directions

1. In a small skillet, heat the oil on medium-low heat and sauté the onion and garlic for about 5 minutes.
2. Stir in the peaches, pear, and honey and cook for about 2 minutes.
3. Season with the curry powder, salt and pepper and simmer for about 5-6 minutes.

VANILLA PEAR
Muffins

Prep Time: 15 mins
Total Time: 1 hr

Servings per Recipe: 12

Calories	240 kcal
Fat	13.4 g
Carbohydrates	28.2g
Protein	3.4 g
Cholesterol	16 mg
Sodium	171 mg

Ingredients

1 C. whole wheat flour
1/2 C. all-purpose flour
3/4 C. white sugar
1 1/2 tsp baking powder
1/2 tsp salt
1/2 C. low-fat vanilla yogurt
1/2 C. canola oil
1 egg

2 tsp vanilla extract
1 ripe pear - peeled, cored, and diced
1/2 C. chopped pecans

Directions

1. Set your oven to 450 degrees F before doing anything else and line 12 cups of a muffin tray with the paper liners.
2. In a bowl, mix together the flours, sugar, baking powder and salt.
3. In another bowl, add the yogurt, oil, egg, and vanilla extract and beat till smooth.
4. Add the yogurt mixture into the flour mixture and mix till just combined.
5. Fold in the pear and pecans.
6. Place the mixture into the prepared muffin cups.
7. Place the muffin tray in the oven.
8. Now, set the oven to 350 degrees F.
9. Cook in the oven for about 20-25 minutes or till a toothpick inserted in the center comes out clean.
10. Remove from the oven and let the cake cool in the muffin tray for about 5 minutes.
11. Carefully, invert the muffins onto wire rack to cool completely.

Alternative
Cranberry Sauce

Prep Time: 15 mins
Total Time: 30 mins

Servings per Recipe: 10
Calories	177 kcal
Fat	0.1 g
Carbohydrates	47.3g
Protein	0.4 g
Cholesterol	0 mg
Sodium	2 mg

Ingredients

1/2 C. water
1/2 C. white sugar
2 pears - peeled, cored and diced
1 (12 oz.) package fresh or frozen cranberries

1 C. honey
1 tbsp fresh lemon juice
1 tsp grated lemon zest

Directions

1. In a medium pan, mix together the water and sugar on medium-high heat.
2. Bring to a boil and stir in the pears.
3. Reduce the heat to medium and cook, stirring occasionally for about 3 minutes.
4. Stir in the cranberries and honey and cook for about 5 minutes.
5. Remove from the heat and stir in the lemon juice and lemon zest.
6. Keep aside to cool at room temperature.
7. Store in an airtight jar and refrigerate, covered for up to one week.

COUNTRY
Pear Cobbler

Prep Time: 15 mins
Total Time: 1 hr

Servings per Recipe: 9
Calories	339 kcal
Fat	13.6 g
Carbohydrates	54.9g
Protein	2.4 g
Cholesterol	34 mg
Sodium	100 mg

Ingredients

4 pears, cored and cut into 1/2-inch slices
1 tsp lemon juice
1/3 C. maple syrup
2 tbsp melted butter
Topping:
1 C. rolled oats
1 C. brown sugar

1/2 C. melted butter
1/2 C. all-purpose flour
1 tsp ground cinnamon

Directions

1. Set your oven to 375 degrees F before doing anything else.
2. In a bowl, add the pears and lemon juice and toss to coat.
3. In the bottom of a 9x9-inch baking dish, place the pear mixture.
4. Place the maple syrup and 2 tbsp of the melted butter over the pear mixture and toss to coat.
5. In a bowl, add the oats, brown sugar, 1/2 C. of the melted butter, flour and cinnamon and mix till a crumbly mixture forms.
6. Spread the crumb mixture over the pear mixture evenly.
7. Cook in the oven for about 45 minutes.

Manhattan Lunch Pizza

Prep Time: 10 mins
Total Time: 25 mins

Servings per Recipe: 8
Calories	287 kcal
Fat	12.9 g
Carbohydrates	31g
Protein	11.6 g
Cholesterol	19 mg
Sodium	585 mg

Ingredients

1 (16 oz.) package refrigerated pizza crust dough
4 oz. sliced provolone cheese
1 Bosc pear, thinly sliced
2 oz. chopped walnuts

2 1/2 oz. Gorgonzola cheese, crumbled
2 tbsp chopped fresh chives

Directions

1. Set your oven to 450 degrees F before doing anything else.
2. In a medium baking sheet, arrange the pizza crust.
3. Place the Provolone cheese over the crust.
4. Place the pear slices over the cheese and sprinkle with the walnuts and Gorgonzola cheese.
5. Cook in the oven for about 8-10 minutes.
6. Remove from the heat and top with the chives.
7. Cut into slice and serve.

PEAR
Loaf

Prep Time: 10 mins
Total Time: 1 hr 20 mins

Servings per Recipe: 9
Calories	304 kcal
Fat	15.8 g
Carbohydrates	38.5g
Protein	3.5 g
Cholesterol	28 mg
Sodium	208 mg

Ingredients

1 C. vegetable oil
2 C. granulated sugar
3 eggs
2 1/2 C. pears - peeled, cored and chopped
1 C. chopped pecans
2 tsp vanilla extract
3 C. all-purpose flour

1 tsp baking soda
1 tsp baking powder
1 tsp salt
1 tsp ground cinnamon
1/2 tsp ground nutmeg

Directions

1. Set your oven to 350 degrees F before doing anything else and grease 2 (8x4-inch) loaf pans.
2. In large bowl add the oil, sugar and eggs and beat well.
3. Stir in the pears, pecans and vanilla.
4. In another bowl, mix together the flour, baking soda, baking powder, salt, cinnamon and nutmeg.
5. Add the flour mixture into the pear mixture and mix well.
6. Transfer the mixture in the prepared loaf pans evenly.
7. Cook in the oven for about 60 minutes or till a toothpick inserted in the center comes out clean.
8. Remove from the oven and let the cake cool in the pan for about 10 minutes.
9. Carefully, invert the cakes onto wire rack to cool completely.

Canadian
Pear Crisp

🥣 Prep Time: 15 mins
🕐 Total Time: 1 hr

Servings per Recipe: 8
Calories	303 kcal
Fat	13.7 g
Carbohydrates	45.9g
Protein	2.4 g
Cholesterol	31 mg
Sodium	87 mg

Ingredients

2 Rome Beauty apples - peeled, cored, and cubed
2 Comice pears - peeled, cored, and cubed
1/2 C. dried cranberries
1 tbsp all-purpose flour
2 tbsp honey
1 1/2 tbsp lemon juice
1/2 C. all-purpose flour

1/2 C. packed brown sugar
1/2 C. quick cooking oats
1/4 C. ground walnuts
1/2 C. butter

Directions

1. Set your oven to 375 degrees F before doing anything else and grease an 8-inch baking dish.
2. In the bottom of the prepared baking dish, mix together the apples, pears, cranberries, 1 tbsp of the flour, honey and lemon juice.
3. In a bowl, add 1/2 C. of the flour, brown sugar, oats, walnuts and butter and mix till a coarse crumb forms.
4. Spread the crumb over the fruit mixture.
5. Cook in the oven for about 45 minutes.

SKINNY GIRL'S
Mixed Greens Salad

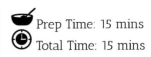

🥣 Prep Time: 15 mins
🕐 Total Time: 15 mins

Servings per Recipe: 6	
Calories	397 kcal
Fat	30.2 g
Cholesterol	25.3g
Sodium	8 g
Carbohydrates	15 mg
Protein	631 mg

Ingredients

1 (10 oz.) bag mixed field greens
1/2 C. sliced red onion
1 Bosc pear, cored and sliced
1/2 C. chopped candied pecans
1/2 C. crumbled blue cheese
1/4 C. maple syrup
1/3 C. apple cider vinegar
1/2 C. mayonnaise

2 tbsp packed brown sugar
3/4 tsp salt
1/4 tsp freshly ground black pepper
1/4 C. walnut oil

Directions

1. In a large bowl, place the salad greens, red onion, pear, pecans and blue cheese and toss to combine.
2. For the dressing in a blender, add the maple syrup, vinegar, mayonnaise, brown sugar, salt and pepper and pulse till well combined.
3. While the motor is running, slowly add the walnut oil and pulse till the mixture becomes creamy.
4. Place the dressing over the salad mixture and toss to coat well.
5. Serve immediately.

Buttery Beets Puree

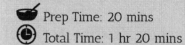

Prep Time: 20 mins
Total Time: 1 hr 20 mins

Servings per Recipe: 6
Calories	220 kcal
Fat	19.1 g
Carbohydrates	13g
Protein	1.2 g
Cholesterol	50 mg
Sodium	132 mg

Ingredients

3 medium beets
5 oz. unsalted butter
1/2 C. minced Vidalia onions
1 1/2 Bosc pears - peeled, cored and minced
2 tsp white sugar

3 tbsp cranberry vinegar
1/4 tsp salt

Directions

1. Set your oven to 400 degrees F before doing anything else.
2. In a roasting pan, place the beets and cook in the oven for about 45-60 minutes.
3. Remove from the oven and keep aside to cool.
4. In a large skillet, melt the butter on medium heat and cook the pears, onion, sugar and vinegar for about 20 minutes, stirring occasionally.
5. After cooling, peel the beets and chop roughly.
6. In a food processor, add the pear mixture and pulse till pureed.
7. Add salt and 1/2 of the beets and pulse about 4-5 times.
8. Add remaining beets and pulse 2-3 times.

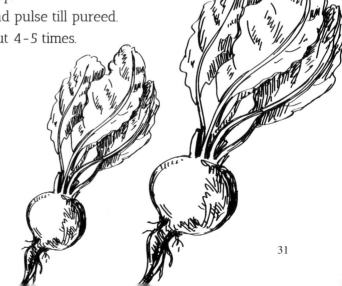

HOMEMADE
Apple Sauce

Prep Time: 15 mins
Total Time: 35 mins

Servings per Recipe: 8

Calories	77 kcal
Fat	0.2 g
Carbohydrates	20.1g
Protein	0.5 g
Cholesterol	0 mg
Sodium	2 mg

Ingredients

4 pears, cut into chunks
3 apples, cut into chunks
1/2 C. water
1 tsp vanilla extract

1/4 tsp ground cinnamon

Directions

1. Heat a skillet over medium heat.
2. Add the pears, apples, water and vanilla extract and simmer, covered for about 10 minutes.
3. Uncover and cook for about 10-15 minutes or till most of the liquid is absorbed.
4. Remove from the heat and keep aside to cool slightly.
5. Transfer the mixture in a food processor and pulse till smooth.
6. Stir in the cinnamon.
7. Serve warm or refrigerate up to 4 days.

Pear Pasta

🥣 Prep Time: 10 mins
🕐 Total Time: 25 mins

Servings per Recipe: 2
Calories	1828 kcal
Fat	68.6 g
Carbohydrates	1236.7g
Protein	73.6 g
Cholesterol	1147 mg
Sodium	712 mg

Ingredients

9 oz. penne pasta
2 tbsp butter
1/2 C. grated Parmesan cheese
3 tbsp crumbled Gorgonzola cheese
1/2 C. heavy whipping cream
1 large pear, peeled and cubed

1/2 C. chopped toasted walnuts
ground black pepper to taste

Directions

1. In large pan of the lightly salted boiling water, cook the pasta for about 11 minutes.
2. Drain well.
3. Return the pasta to the pan and stir in the butter, Parmesan cheese and Gorgonzola cheese on medium heat.
4. Cook till the cheese melts completely.
5. Add the cream into the pasta mixture and stir to combine.
6. Remove from the heat and fold the pear into the pasta mixture.
7. Season with pepper.
8. Serve with a topping of the walnuts.

FORT COLLINS
Fruit Smoothie

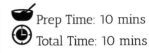

Prep Time: 10 mins
Total Time: 10 mins

Servings per Recipe: 2
Calories 164 kcal
Fat 0.5 g
Cholesterol 36g
Sodium 6 g
Carbohydrates 2 mg
Protein 71 mg

Ingredients

1/2 C. ice
1 Asian pear, cored and cubed
2 large strawberries, hulled
2/3 C. vanilla fat-free yogurt

1/4 C. fat-free milk
2 tsp white sugar

Directions

1. In a blender, add all the ingredients and pulse till smooth.

Milanese Bruschetta

🥣 Prep Time: 10 mins
🕐 Total Time: 15 mins

Servings per Recipe: 8	
Calories	315 kcal
Fat	12.8 g
Carbohydrates	36.6g
Protein	13.5 g
Cholesterol	27 mg
Sodium	933 mg

Ingredients

1 pear, cored and diced
1/3 C. diced red onion
1 tbsp olive oil
1 tbsp balsamic vinegar
1 tbsp chopped fresh thyme
1 (4 oz.) package crumbled blue cheese

1 French baguette, sliced and toasted
1/3 lb. sliced prosciutto, cut into thin strips

Directions

1. In a large bowl, mix together the pear, onion, olive oil, balsamic vinegar and thyme and keep aside to marinate for about 5 minutes.
2. Spread the blue cheese over the toasted baguette slices.
3. Place the pear mixture over the blue cheese evenly and top with the prosciutto.

MY LUNCH BOX
Sandwich

Prep Time: 10 mins
Total Time: 15 mins

Servings per Recipe: 1

Calories	670 kcal
Fat	41.3 g
Carbohydrates	56.5g
Protein	22 g
Cholesterol	121 mg
Sodium	1386 mg

Ingredients

2 tbsp butter, softened
2 thick slices French bread
6 thin slices Brie cheese, or more to taste
12 fresh thyme leaves, or to taste

1 pinch cracked black pepper
6 slices pear (such as Bosc)
salt to taste

Directions

1. Spread the butter on one side of each bread slice generously.
2. Heat a skillet on medium heat.
3. Place bread slices butter-side down into hot skillet.
4. Place the Brie cheese slices on top of each bread slice and sprinkle with the thyme and cracked black pepper.
5. Arrange the pear slices in a single layer over the Brie cheese on one slice of bread and sprinkle with a pinch of the salt.
6. Place the slice of bread without pears onto the slice of bread with the pear slices.
7. Cook for about 2-3 minutes per side.
8. Transfer to a plate and cut into halves.

Sweet
Potato Pan

🥣 Prep Time: 20 mins
🕐 Total Time: 1 hr 35 mins

Servings per Recipe: 8
Calories	405 kcal
Fat	18.2 g
Carbohydrates	58.2g
Protein	5.9 g
Cholesterol	24 mg
Sodium	151 mg

Ingredients

8 sweet potatoes
4 pears - peeled, cored and chopped
1 C. evaporated milk
2 tsp vanilla extract
1/2 C. packed brown sugar
4 tbsp butter

1/2 tsp ground cinnamon
1 pinch freshly grated nutmeg
2 tbsp orange juice
1 C. chopped pecans

Directions

1. Set your oven to 350 degrees F before doing anything else.
2. With a fork, prick the sweet potatoes and cook in the oven for about 1 hour.
3. Remove from the oven and peel the baked sweet potatoes.
4. Place the sweet potatoes in a medium bowl and whip until smooth.
5. In a medium pan, add the pears on medium heat and gently cook or about 10 minutes.
6. Transfer the pears in a food processor and pulse till smooth.
7. In a medium pan, mix together the evaporated milk, vanilla, brown sugar and butter on medium heat.
8. Heat till scalded and then blend into the sweet potatoes.
9. Add the pear puree, cinnamon, nutmeg, orange juice and pecans into the sweet potato mixture and mix well.
10. Transfer the mixture into a large baking dish.
11. Cook in the oven for about 15 minutes.

MINCEMEAT
Pears for Brunch

🥣 Prep Time: 30 mins
🕐 Total Time: 50 mins

Servings per Recipe: 96	
Calories	102 kcal
Fat	0.1 g
Carbohydrates	26.6g
Protein	0.5 g
Cholesterol	0 mg
Sodium	26 mg

Ingredients

6 C. white sugar
1 tsp ground cinnamon
1 tsp ground allspice
1 tsp ground cloves
1 tsp salt
8 lb. pears - peeled, cored and chopped
1 large orange, quartered with peel
1 lemon, quartered and seeded
1 tart apple - peeled, cored and

chopped
1 C. dried apricots, chopped
1 C. grape juice
1 C. cider vinegar
3 C. raisins
2 1/2 C. dried currants

Directions

1. In a large pan, mix together the sugar, cinnamon, allspice, cloves and salt.
2. Into the same pan, add the pears, orange, lemon, apple and apricot.
3. With a potato masher, mash the fruit mixture.
4. Stir in the grape juice, vinegar, raisins, and currants on medium heat and bring to a boil, stirring occasionally.
5. Simmer, uncovered till thick.
6. Transfer the mixture into hot sterilized jars to within 1/4 inch of jar top and seal tightly.

Fruity
Tortillas Bowls

🥣 Prep Time: 30 mins

⏱ Total Time: 1 hr

Servings per Recipe: 6

Calories	746 kcal
Fat	35.2 g
Carbohydrates	104.3g
Protein	9.2 g
Cholesterol	39 mg
Sodium	349 mg

Ingredients

4 Bartlett pears, cored and diced
1/2 C. white sugar
1 tbsp cornstarch
2 tsp ground cinnamon
1 tsp lemon zest
1/2 C. graham cracker crumbs
1/2 C. chopped pecans
1 quart vanilla ice cream
6 (8 inch) flour tortillas

1 quart vegetable oil for frying
1/4 C. honey
1 tsp ground cinnamon
1 tbsp white sugar

Directions

1. For the tortilla shells in a deep fryer, heat the oil to 375 degrees F.
2. Gently, place one tortilla in the hot oil, pressing the center with a wooden spoon till the tortilla forms a cup.
3. Gently turn and fry each tortilla separately until golden brown on both sides.
4. In a pan, mix together the pears, sugar, cornstarch, 1 tsp of the cinnamon and lemon zest on medium heat.
5. Bring to a boil, stirring continuously and cook for about 1 minute.
6. Remove from the heat and keep aside to cool.
7. In a bowl, mix together the cookie crumbs, pecans and remaining cinnamon.
8. Form ice cream into 4-6 balls and coat with the crumb mixture evenly.
9. Arrange an ice cream ball in each fried tortilla shell.
10. Top with the cooled pear mixture.
11. Fried tortilla shells can be brushed with honey and dusted with ground cinnamon and sugar before filling, if desired.

ALTERNATIVE
Poached Pears

Prep Time: 15 mins
Total Time: 35 mins

Servings per Recipe: 8
Calories	129 kcal
Fat	4 g
Carbohydrates	20.3g
Protein	0.7 g
Cholesterol	11 mg
Sodium	29 mg

Ingredients

4 Bartlett pears, about 8 oz. each, halved
lengthwise and cored
1/2 C. Holland House(R) Marsala
Cooking Wine
2 tbsp packed brown sugar
1 tsp vanilla extract
1/4 tsp cinnamon
1/8 tsp nutmeg
2 tbsp butter

Vanilla ice cream
Toasted pecans

Directions

1. In a small bowl, add the cooking wine, brown sugar, vanilla, cinnamon and nutmeg and stir till the sugar is dissolved.
2. In a large 12-inch skillet, melt the butter on medium heat.
3. Stir in the wine mixture and cook till bubbly.
4. Place pears in pan, cut side down and reduce the heat to medium-low.
5. Cook, covered for about 20 minutes.
6. Remove from the heat and keep aside for about 30-45 minutes to cool enough to serve.
7. Place each pear half in a small bowl.
8. Stir the remaining sauce in the pan.
9. Pour about 1-2 tsp of the warm sauce over each serving.
10. Top with a small scoop of ice cream and toasted pecans and serve immediately.

My First
Pear Tartlets

🥣 Prep Time: 15 mins
🕐 Total Time: 30 mins

Servings per Recipe: 24
Calories	48 kcal
Fat	2.3 g
Carbohydrates	5g
Protein	1.5 g
Cholesterol	5 mg
Sodium	40 mg

Ingredients

24 mini phyllo tart shells
1/4 lb. ripe Brie cheese, cut into 24 small chunks
1 ripe pear, cut into small dice
2 sprigs fresh thyme

2 tbsp honey, or to taste

Directions

1. Set your oven to 400 degrees F before doing anything else and line a jelly roll pan with parchment paper.
2. Place the tart shells onto the prepared pan.
3. Arrange a piece of the Brie cheese into each shell.
4. Place the diced pear and a couple thyme leaves into each shell and drizzle with the honey.
5. Cook in the oven for about 12-15 minutes.

SWEET
& Tangy Glazed Pears

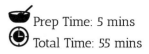 Prep Time: 5 mins

Total Time: 55 mins

Servings per Recipe: 16

Calories	115 kcal
Fat	2.8 g
Carbohydrates	24.2g
Protein	0.4 g
Cholesterol	10 mg
Sodium	4 mg

Ingredients

4 Bosc pears - peeled, cored, and quartered
1 C. honey, divided
1 1/2 C. fig preserves
1/2 C. pomegranate molasses

1 pinch ground cinnamon
1/2 C. heavy cream
1/4 tsp almond extract

Directions

1. Set your oven to 375 degrees F before doing anything else and grease a baking sheet.
2. Place the pear quarters on the prepared baking sheet in a single layer.
3. Drizzle the honey over the pears, reserving about 1 tbsp of the honey.
4. In a small pan, mix together the fig preserves, pomegranate molasses and cinnamon on medium heat.
5. Bring to a boil and reduce the heat to low to keep at a simmer till ready to use
6. Cook the pears in the oven for about 15-20 minutes.
7. Now, set the oven to 325 degrees F.
8. Coat the pears with the fig glaze and cook in the oven for about 25-35 minutes more.
9. Remove from the oven and keep aside to cool for about 5 minutes.
10. Meanwhile, in a large glass bowl, add the cream, almond extract and reserved honey and with a hand mixer, beat till thick.
11. Serve the pears with a dollop of the whipped cream mixture.

Poaced Pears in Brussels

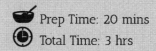
Prep Time: 20 mins
Total Time: 3 hrs

Servings per Recipe: 4
Calories	1060 kcal
Fat	13.5 g
Carbohydrates	240.9g
Protein	4.2 g
Cholesterol	15 mg
Sodium	252 mg

Ingredients

6 C. water
1 lemon, zested and juiced
4 Bosc pears - cored, peeled, stems left on
1 vanilla bean, split lengthwise and scrape out the seeds

3 C. sugar
1 C. prepared hot fudge topping, or as needed
1 C. vanilla ice cream, or as needed

Directions

1. In a heavy pan, mix together the water, sugar, seeds and split pods of the vanilla bean and zest and juice of 1 lemon on medium heat.
2. Place the pears in the pan.
3. Bring to a simmer, stirring gently to dissolve the sugar.
4. Reduce the heat so the pears can cook on a steady, gentle simmer.
5. Pears need to stay submerged, so place a small plate over them in the pot to keep them under the liquid. Simmer for about 20 - 25 minutes.
6. Remove the pan from the heat and keep aside to cool the pears at room temperature in the poaching liquid.
7. Transfer the pears and vanilla beans to a storage container and cover with some of the poaching liquid.
8. Reserve the remaining poaching liquid.
9. Refrigerate, covered for overnight or till the pears are chilled completely.
10. In a pan, heat the hot fudge sauce on medium heat till warm.
11. Dip the base of the pears into the chocolate and spoon chocolate along the sides except for the top.
12. Place the dipped pears in individual serving bowls with another generous spoonful of the syrup and a small scoop of the vanilla ice cream.

BUTTERNUT PEAR
Soup

Prep Time: 15 mins
Total Time: 1 hr 45 mins

Servings per Recipe: 8

Calories	167 kcal
Fat	6.6 g
Carbohydrates	27.5g
Protein	3 g
Cholesterol	20 mg
Sodium	786 mg

Ingredients

1 (2 lb.) butternut squash
3 tbsp unsalted butter
1 onion, diced
2 cloves garlic, minced
2 tsp minced fresh ginger root
1 tbsp curry powder
1 tsp salt
4 C. reduced sodium chicken broth

2 firm ripe Bartlett pears, peeled, cored, and cut into 1 inch dice
1/2 C. half and half

Directions

1. Set your oven to 375 degrees F before doing anything else and line a rimmed baking sheet with parchment paper.
2. Cut the squash in half lengthwise and discard the seeds and membrane.
3. Place squash halves, cut sides down on the prepared baking sheet.
4. Cook in the oven for about 45 minutes.
5. Scoop the pulp from the peel and reserve.
6. In a large soup pan, melt butter on medium heat and cook the onion, garlic, ginger, curry powder and salt for about 10 minutes.
7. Add the chicken broth and bring to a boil.
8. Stir in the pears and the reserved squash and simmer for about 30 minutes.
9. Remove from the heat and keep aside to cool slightly.
10. In a blender, add the soup in batches and pulse till smooth.
11. Return the soup to the pan and stir in the half and half.
12. Cook till heated completely.

Pomodoro
Pears

🥣 Prep Time: 10 mins
🕐 Total Time: 10 mins

Servings per Recipe: 4
Calories	164 kcal
Fat	1.9 g
Cholesterol	38.9g
Sodium	1.7 g
Carbohydrates	0 mg
Protein	5 mg

Ingredients

3 pears - peeled, cored and cut into wedges
1 pomegranate, skin and light-colored membrane removed
1 tbsp fresh lemon juice
2 tbsp light brown sugar
1/4 tsp ground nutmeg

1/2 tsp ground cinnamon
2 tbsp finely chopped almonds (optional)
4 sprigs fresh mint leaves for garnish (optional)

Directions

1. In a bowl, place the sliced pears, pomegranate seeds and lemon juice and toss to coat well.
2. In a small bowl, mix together the brown sugar, nutmeg and cinnamon.
3. Add the brown sugar mixture into the bowl with the fruit and gently, stir to combine.
4. Refrigerate, covered for at least 1 hour before serving.
5. Serve with a garnishing of the chopped almonds and a sprig of mint.

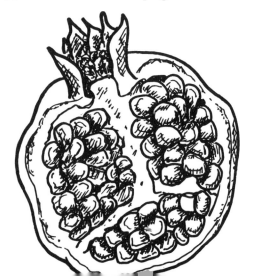

BALSAMIC CHICKEN
with Pears and Veggies

Prep Time: 20 mins
Total Time: 4 hrs 20 mins

Servings per Recipe: 4
Calories	309 kcal
Fat	7.4 g
Carbohydrates	33.5g
Protein	29.1 g
Cholesterol	69 mg
Sodium	70 mg

Ingredients

1 tbsp vegetable oil
4 skinless, boneless chicken breast
halves, cut into strips
1 onion, sliced thin
salt and ground black pepper to taste
2 ripe Bartlett pears, cored and sliced
1 lb. fresh asparagus, trimmed
4 cloves garlic, minced

2 tbsp balsamic vinegar
3 tbsp apple juice
1 tsp dried rosemary
1 tbsp grated fresh ginger
2 tbsp dark brown sugar

Directions

1. In a skillet, heat oil on medium heat.
2. Add the chicken and cook for about 3-5 minutes.
3. Transfer the chicken into a slow cooker.
4. Add the onion, salt and pepper and top with the pears and asparagus.
5. In a bowl, mix together the garlic, balsamic vinegar, apple juice, rosemary, ginger and sugar.
6. Place the vinegar mixture on top and again season with the salt and pepper.
7. Set the slow cooker on Low.
8. Cover and cook for about 4-6 hours.

Packed
Pear Cookies

Prep Time: 30 mins
Total Time: 50 mins

Servings per Recipe: 15

Calories	299 kcal
Fat	9.2 g
Carbohydrates	52.9g
Protein	3 g
Cholesterol	29 mg
Sodium	104 mg

Ingredients

1/2 C. butter, softened
1 1/2 C. packed brown sugar
1 egg
1 tsp vanilla extract
2 C. all-purpose flour
1 1/2 tsp baking powder
1 tsp ground cinnamon
1 tsp ground ginger

1 pear - peeled, cored and diced
1/2 C. raisins
1/2 C. chopped walnuts
1 1/2 C. confectioners' sugar
2 1/2 tbsp lemon juice

Directions

1. Set your oven to 350 degrees F before doing anything else.
2. In large bowl, add the butter and sugar and beat till smooth.
3. Add the egg and vanilla and beat well.
4. In another bowl, mix together the flour, baking powder, cinnamon and ginger.
5. Place the mixture with a rounded tbsp onto the baking sheets.
6. Cook in the oven for about 15 minutes.
7. Remove from the oven and place onto the wire racks to cool.
8. In a bowl, add the confectioners' sugar and lemon juice and mix till smooth.
9. Spoon the icing over the cookies before serving.

ROXY'S
Yogurt

🥣 Prep Time: 5 mins
🕐 Total Time: 45 mins

Servings per Recipe: 8
Calories	111 kcal
Fat	0.8 g
Cholesterol	23.7g
Sodium	3.2 g
Carbohydrates	3 mg
Protein	43 mg

Ingredients

1 (15 oz.) can pear halves
2 C. vanilla yogurt
1/3 C. white sugar
1/2 tsp ground cinnamon

1/4 tsp ground allspice

Directions

1. Drain the ca of the pears, reserving 1/2 C. of the juice.
2. In a food processor, add the pears and pulse till pureed.
3. In an ice-cream maker mix together the pears, reserved juice, yogurt, sugar, cinnamon and allspice and freeze according to manufacturers' directions.

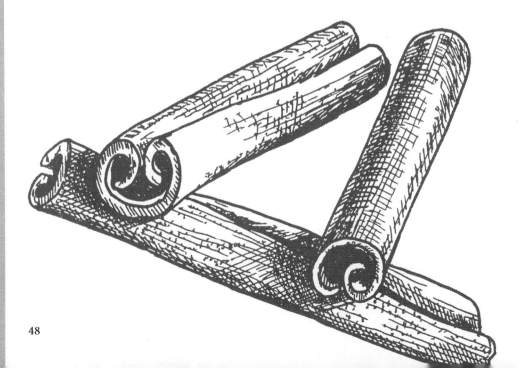

Pear Bites

🥣 Prep Time: 35 mins
🕐 Total Time: 2 hrs

Servings per Recipe: 36
Calories   109 kcal
Fat   7.4 g
Carbohydrates   9.2g
Protein   1.8 g
Cholesterol   5 mg
Sodium   91 mg

Ingredients

3 tbsp butter
1 tbsp olive oil
4 sweet onions, thinly sliced
salt and pepper to taste

1 (17.5 oz.) package frozen puff pastry, thawed
2 firm pears, peeled, quartered, and sliced
3/4 C. crumbled blue cheese

Directions

1. Set your oven to 375 degrees F before doing anything else and line two baking sheets with parchment papers.
2. In a skillet, melt the butter and olive oil on medium heat.
3. Add the onions and cook, stirring occasionally for about 30-40 minutes.
4. Season with the salt and pepper and remove from the heat, then keep aside to cool.
5. With a sharp knife, cut each sheet of the puff pastry into 9 squares.
6. Cut each square in half diagonally to make 36 triangles.
7. Arrange the triangles onto the prepared baking sheets and top with the caramelized onions, pears and 1 tsp of blue cheese.
8. Cook in the oven for about 20-30 minutes.

NUTTY
Pear Casserole

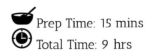 Prep Time: 15 mins
Total Time: 9 hrs

Servings per Recipe: 20
Calories	192 kcal
Fat	6.7 g
Carbohydrates	26g
Protein	7.5 g
Cholesterol	121 mg
Sodium	215 mg

Ingredients

1/4 C. butter, cut into 1/4-inch cubes
1/2 C. brown sugar
1 (29 oz.) can pear halves, cut
lengthwise into 4 slices
1 (1 lb.) loaf sourdough bread, cut into
1-inch cubes
2 1/2 C. eggs
1 1/2 C. milk

2 tbsp white sugar
1 tsp vanilla extract
1/2 tsp almond extract
1/4 C. sliced almonds

Directions

1. In the bottom of a 14x10-inch baking dish, place the butter cubes evenly.
2. Sprinkle the brown sugar over the butter evenly.
3. Arrange the pear slices over the butter cubes evenly.
4. Place the bread cubes over the pear slices into a single layer.
5. In a bowl, add the eggs, milk, sugar, vanilla extract and almond extract and mix till fully.
6. Place the mixture over the bread cubes evenly.
7. With some foil, cover the dish and refrigerate to chill for overnight.
8. Set your oven to 350 degrees F.
9. Remove the baking dish from the refrigerator and keep aside to warm while the oven preheats.
10. Cook in the oven for about 40-60 minutes.
11. Serve with a topping of the sliced almonds.

Simple Pear and Apple Crumble

🥣 Prep Time: 20 mins
🕐 Total Time: 1 hr

Servings per Recipe: 8
Calories	366 kcal
Fat	15.7 g
Carbohydrates	55g
Protein	4.5 g
Cholesterol	31 mg
Sodium	91 mg

Ingredients

1 1/2 C. rolled oats
1/2 C. all-purpose flour
3/4 C. brown sugar
1/2 C. butter, softened
2 C. peeled and diced apples
2 C. peeled and diced pears
3/4 C. brown sugar
1 tsp ground cinnamon

1/2 C. sliced almonds, or to taste

Directions

1. Set your oven to 350 degrees F before doing anything else.
2. In a bowl, add the oats, flour, 3/4 C. of the brown sugar and butter and mix till the mixture becomes crumbly.
3. In another bowl, mix together the apples, pears, 3/4 C. of the brown sugar and cinnamon.
4. In the bottom of a 9x9-inch glass pan, place the fruit mixture evenly.
5. Sprinkle the oat mixture over the fruit mixture and top with the almonds.
6. Cook in the oven for about 40 minutes.

PEAR
and Blackberry
Crumble

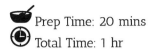

Prep Time: 20 mins
Total Time: 1 hr

Servings per Recipe: 18
Calories	185 kcal
Fat	7.7 g
Carbohydrates	29.1g
Protein	2.2 g
Cholesterol	0 mg
Sodium	115 mg

Ingredients

2 C. whole wheat flour
1 1/2 C. low-fat margarine
1 C. white sugar
3 apples - peeled, cored, and cut into wedges

3 pears - peeled, cored, and cut into wedges
1 C. blackberries

Directions

1. Set your oven to 350 degrees F before doing anything else and grease 3 (9-inch) pie dishes.
2. In a bowl, add the flour, margarine and sugar and mix till the mixture becomes crumbly.
3. In the bottom of the prepared pie dishes, arrange the apples and pears evenly.
4. Place the blackberries over the apples and pears.
5. Sprinkle the flour mixture over the fruit mixture evenly.
6. Cook in the oven for about 40 minutes.

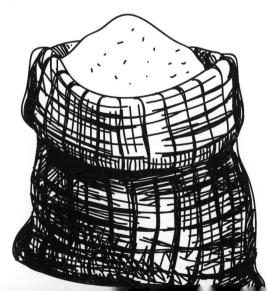

Lisa's Gourmet
Pear Crisp

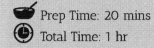 Prep Time: 20 mins
Total Time: 1 hr

Servings per Recipe: 6
Calories	449 kcal
Fat	13.8 g
Carbohydrates	80.8g
Protein	5.6 g
Cholesterol	40 mg
Sodium	97 mg

Ingredients

1 C. rolled oats
1/3 C. brown sugar
1/2 C. all-purpose flour
1 tsp finely chopped crystallized ginger
1 tsp ground cinnamon
1/4 C. butter
2 tbsp white sugar
2 tbsp all-purpose flour

2 tsp finely chopped crystallized ginger
8 C. peeled and sliced pears
1 pint vanilla ice cream

Directions

1. Set your oven to 375 degrees F before doing anything else and grease a 9-inch square baking dish.
2. In a medium bowl, mix together the oats, brown sugar, 1/2 C. of the flour, 1 tsp of the crystallized ginger and cinnamon.
3. Add the butter and mix till the mixture becomes crumbly.
4. In another bowl, mix together the white sugar, 2 tbsp of the flour and 2 tsp of the crystallized ginger.
5. Add the sliced pears and toss to coat.
6. Transfer the mixture into the prepared baking dish.
7. Spread the oat topping over the top evenly.
8. Cook in the oven for about 30 to 35 minutes.
9. Cool slightly before serving with the vanilla ice cream.

GORMET
Birthday Cake 101

🥣 Prep Time: 20 mins
🕐 Total Time: 1 hr 20 mins

Servings per Recipe: 16	
Calories	283 kcal
Fat	14.7 g
Carbohydrates	36g
Protein	3.3 g
Cholesterol	52 mg
Sodium	274 mg

Ingredients

3 eggs
1 1/3 C. applesauce
3 tbsp molasses
1/2 C. butter, melted
1 (18.5 oz.) package yellow cake mix
2 tsp ground cinnamon
1 tsp ground nutmeg
1/4 tsp ground cloves

1 tbsp finely shredded orange peel
1 small Bosc pear, peeled and thinly
sliced
1/2 C. pecans, chopped
1 (2.6 oz.) bar milk chocolate, coarsely
chopped

Directions

1. Set your oven to 350 degrees F before doing anything else and grease and flour a 10-inch spring-form pan.
2. In a large bowl, add the eggs, applesauce, molasses, and butter and beat till well combined.
3. Add the cake mix, cinnamon, nutmeg, cloves, and orange peel and beat on medium speed for about 4 minutes.
4. Transfer the mixture into the prepared pan.
5. Top with the pear slices and sprinkle with the pecans and chopped chocolate.
6. Cook in the oven for about 55-60 minutes or till a toothpick inserted in the center comes out clean.
7. Remove from the oven and let the cake cool in the pan for about 25 minutes.

October's
Pear Pie

Prep Time: 20 mins
Total Time: 1 hr

Servings per Recipe: 8

Calories	418 kcal
Fat	18.5 g
Carbohydrates	62.7g
Protein	3.9 g
Cholesterol	1 mg
Sodium	4920 mg

Ingredients

1 Classic Crisco(R) Double Pie Crust
4 C. peeled, thinly sliced pears
2 C. peeled, thinly sliced apples
3/4 C. sugar
2 tbsp Pillsbury BEST(R) All Purpose Flour
3/4 tsp ground cinnamon
3/4 tsp ground ginger
1/4 tsp salt

1 tbsp lemon juice
Milk
Cinnamon sugar

Directions

1. Set your oven to 400 degrees F before doing anything else.
2. Prepare the recipe for the double crust pie.
3. Roll out the dough for the bottom crust.
4. Arrange in a 9-inch pie plate and press to fit without stretching dough.
5. Trim even with pie plate.
6. In a large bowl, mix together the pears, apples, flour, sugar, cinnamon, ginger, salt and lemon juice.
7. Transfer the mixture into the prepared pie crust.
8. Roll out the dough for the top crust.
9. Cut into strips creating a lattice top and trim 1/2-inch beyond the edge.
10. Fold under the bottom crust edge to seal.
11. Crimp and flute the edges.
12. Cut slits in top crust to allow steam to escape.
13. Coat the crust with milk and sprinkle with the cinnamon sugar.
14. Cook in the oven for about 30-40 minutes.

FULL
Pear Cake

🥣 Prep Time: 20 mins
🕐 Total Time: 1 hr 55 mins

Servings per Recipe: 16	
Calories	438 kcal
Fat	25.4 g
Carbohydrates	50.8g
Protein	4.1 g
Cholesterol	50 mg
Sodium	279 mg

Ingredients

2 C. all-purpose flour
1 tsp baking soda
1 tsp salt
1 tsp ground cinnamon
1/2 tsp ground nutmeg
1 1/2 C. white sugar
3 eggs
1 C. vegetable oil
1 tsp vanilla extract
2 C. peeled and diced pears

1 C. chopped walnuts
Brown Butter Icing:
1/2 C. butter
2 C. confectioners' sugar
1 tsp vanilla extract
3 tbsp water

Directions

1. Set your oven to 350 degrees F before doing anything else and grease and flour a 10-inch tube pan.
2. In a large bowl, mix together the flour, baking soda, cinnamon, nutmeg and salt.
3. In another bowl, add the sugar and eggs and with an electric mixer on medium speed, beat till light and fluffy.
4. Add the oil and 1 tsp of the vanilla extract and beat till well combined.
5. Add the flour mixture and mix till the mixture becomes smooth.
6. Fold in the pears and walnuts.
7. Transfer the mixture in the prepared cake pan evenly.
8. Cook in the oven for about 50-55 minutes or till a toothpick inserted in the center comes out clean.
9. Remove from the oven and let the cake cool in the pan for about 10 minutes.
10. Carefully, invert the cakes onto wire rack to cool completely.

11. For icing in a pan, melt the butter on medium-low heat, stirring continuously.
12. For icing in a pan, melt the butter on medium-low heat, stirring continuously.
13. Cook, stirring continuously for about 5 minutes.
14. Remove from the heat and add the confectioners' sugar and 1 tsp of the vanilla extract and mix till the icing becomes thick and smooth.
15. Stir in the water, 1 tbsp at a time to thin the icing to desired consistency.
16. Drizzle icing over the cooled cake.

ENJOY THE RECIPES?

KEEP ON COOKING
WITH 6 MORE FREE COOKBOOKS!

Visit our website and simply enter your email address to join the club and receive your 6 cookbooks.

http://booksumo.com/magnet

https://www.instagram.com/booksumopress/

https://www.facebook.com/booksumo/